THE MOST INSPIRING BOOK ON GENERATING WEALTH FOR THE AVERAGE PERSON EVER WRITTEN.

MAKING MILLIONS

From Thought to Reality

THE MODERN-DAY BIBLE FOR NEW INVESTORS

JOSHUA MATTHEW CHRONICLES,
MSC, BSC, NP
(MILLIONAIRE SUCCESS EXPERT)

MAKING MILLIONS

From Thought to Reality

JOSHUA MATTHEW CHRONICLES,
MSC, BSC, NP

ISBN # 978-1-68593-048-6

Additional copies of this book are available from the Author.

Joshua Matthew Chronicles, P.O. Box 1281 New Llano LA, 71461
MakingmillionsbyJoshua@gmail.com - (325)280-3240

WISE PUBLICATIONS
CUSTOM BOOK MANUFACTURING SINCE 1982
www.wisepublications.biz

809 East Napoleon St. - Sulphur, Louisiana 70663 | 337-527-8308 | wisepublications@yahoo.com

Visit our online Bookstore! www.wisepublications.biz

ACKNOWLEDGEMENTS

This book is laid out in chronological order with ways to make money on the financial market. Within this book is all the enigma you need with the know how to begin unlocking the wealth generating potential and becoming the successful person you were destined to be. The financial market has made massive wealth for an unsurmountable amount of people; it made them extremely wealthy. These steps have been put to the test by countless individuals and if properly taught and understood it can bring in mountains of wealth for you.

The blueprint I am referring to is what I have mentioned on several occasions, throughout the book. Many of you may not know, the gold mine is in your possession already. All those who are searching and are ready to gain this vast wealth of knowledge need not look any further, you have just found it.

All wealthy and successful people in the world today have found this treasure and have used it to generate massive wealth. Success comes before making money; money is just the result of being successful. Reading this book of knowledge and facts, MAKING MILLIONS

FROM THOUGHTS TO REALITY will give you the foundation to begin and the groundwork to build. It is for beginners seeking an understanding of the financial market and also how the economy works. It also entails how money really works and how to work to create assets which will pay you.

Schools whether college or universities never tell you about money and what success is really about. Success is really the progressive realization of a dignitary ideal. We become what we think about. Historically, whatever you think about that's who you are. You can decide who, what, how, where and when about your life endeavors today. You must begin by doing what is of most importance and that is generating your thoughts. Thinking is up to you, the individual.

Ideas are the greatest things on earth, they are the things that change our minds. The future represents great prospects for the individuals who have positive thoughts and ideas and who work towards their goals. Survival should never be the only option for human beings it is of utmost importance as we enjoy our time on earth. When someone succeeds everyone benefits, your family, friends, the community, and it goes on and on.

TABLE OF CONTENTS

THE PENNY

To be born in today's world lacking sufficient money to live at a standard considered comfortable or normal in our society is never your fault but to go through life and not make a difference and die poor is totally and absolutely your fault. It doesn't matter where you're coming from but where you are going. Trading on the financial market is a way I found that took me out of destitution and the 9-5 work cycle sacrificing my time for money and giving away the power or right to act, speak, or think as I wanted without hindrance and restraint and doing what the general public wanted me to do, work until I am 65 then retire then live off my retirement for 10 years or less and die. According to the rules of logic and formal argument, it never made any sense to me, sacrificing my time which is so precious, that its value cannot be determined and it's something that when gone I can never get back, so I made an important decision in my life to find a way out of this pattern and I was introduced to financial trading, that's when my life turned around even before I started making money just doing it made me feel free. This book is concise and straight to the point, it is quite short and hands on. Reading this book, MAKING MILLIONS FROM THOUGHTS TO REALITY and it will be the beginning of the creation of your foundation and the groundwork for beginners in trading whether stock, bonds or crypto and also how the economy work, how money really works and how to work to create assets which will pay you. Schools whether college or universities never tell you about money and what success is really about. Success is really the progressive realization of a dignitary ideal. The opposite of courage in our world today is conformity and compliance with societies standards, everyone acting and adhering to everyone else, we are in the richest land ever known to man and most people in the United States of America are finding it laborious to make ends meet. The only person who achieves the desired aim or result is the one who is realizing a dignitary ideal and who is working towards a goal or a number of goals daily until they are attained. We begin to be what we think about, this word is inspired by God the creator of the universe, the Alpha, and the Omega "so as a man thinketh so his he and has he continues to think so he will remain" If you wish to be good, wealthy and have a good life you can have it. We begin to be what we think about, constructive thoughts and goal-oriented thoughts with an idea of how to carry out an action. The human mind, the most valuable asset we have that enables us to be aware of the world and their experiences, to think, and to feel; the faculty of consciousness and thought is the most valuable asset in our lifetime, it is invaluable and priceless, it can do any job you want it to do and to be anything you want but you have to learn how to control it, plant it in your mind, work towards it and it will happen with the help of God. Matthew Chapter 7:7-11 Ask, and it shall be given you; seek, and ye shall find; knock, and it shall be opened unto you: For everyone that ask receiveth; and he that seeketh findeth; and to him that knocketh it shall be opened. Or what man is there of you, whom if his son ask bread, will he give him stone? Or if he asks for a fish, will he give him a serpent? If ye then, being evil, know how to give good gifts unto your children, how much more shall your Father which is in heaven give good things to them that ask him? Therefore, you must reap what you sow, if you sow positive thoughts, you will gain positive results and conversely for negative thoughts. Sir Isaac Newton's third law of motion to every action there is an opposite and equal reaction this statement which simply means that in every interaction, whether positive or negative there will be a opposite reaction. Everything begins with an idea, making millions of dollars, creating wealth, and having success begins with thoughts and a goal or goals with a plan of action, if you know what you want and enough muster to control your mind you can achieve all you wish for. Financial trading is an intellectual game, it is a very serious intellectual business, your main aim is to take money from other emotional financial traders. Financial day trading is not playing the lotto or gambling in a casino it is a very intellectual game like chess, it is a profession just like a doctor and a lawyer. If you want to be an entrepreneur and run your own business, trading is the perfect start to doing this, buying, and selling daily while profiting and mastering your emotions. The lifestyle of financial day trading is very attractive but there is more to it, this is a skill which will guarantee you financial freedom, you will never sell your time for money anymore. Financial trading is much about psychology, and it is the most important aspect of trading when to get in and get out and not be controlled by your emotions that is really 95% of trading the rest is really watching business news and the type of financial assets you trade. Financial traders must remain objective, professionals trade against a deviation, sell short when a breakout upside is there and buy when too many buyers are in the market and the trade is touching the ceiling. Financial trading is much like riding a bicycle once you learn to do it is a skill no one can take from you. The goal of any professional in any field whether a lawyer, doctor, journalist, or financial trader you must be the best at what you do, the money is really just an afterthought, and it will come once you hone and master your skill. Create a trading system and stick to it, being an emotional trader is the biggest enemy of any trader in trading. The perfect trading system does exist, I will share my trading system in this book that worked for me, how I made it from being homeless to generating massive wealth. Money is essential for survival in today's world, in 100's of years gone by, man could go and hunt for food, but growing up and going to school we were never really taught about money, we were only taught to go to school and get good grades but not how to survive in the real world. The education system teaches you to work a job, work for money. The startup of MAKING MILLIONS FROM THOUGHTS TO REALITY is that you become what you think of most of the time, it won't happen by accident, this book is carefully designed to teach you how to take control of your time and have total freedom. The largest part of successful trading is mastering your mind, emotions, and thoughts. Financial trading demands a certain amount of time and concentration. It is no surprise that more than 75% of all-day traders quit within just two years of trading, 90% of traders lose money, with my strategy followed correctly you will be in the top 10%. My financial trading system is rigid, and I always stick to it to minimize my lost and maximize my profit. If you can make 25% profit a year in profit you will be the king of trading, take this into mind when trading to keep your trading portfolio consistent by maximizing your profit and minimizing your loss. In my trading account I have a 1% rule where I never trade less than 1% of my account. This enhances my profit potential and this 2% limits me and cut down my risk taking on trading stocks. The wealthiest people of the world if you look at history and in our present world search for and build networks; everyone else looks for a job. My main goal in trading is to make the best trade on the stock market, not count my money while I am working. I devote my energy at making the best trade, not focusing on the money, finding good entry points and not the money. Looking for the right trade you must look for market structure and support and resistance, buying stocks when they are on sale. I see many people will go get student loans and accrue significant debt in upwards of $100,000 or more but would never invest $100 in the stock market saying it's too risky and it is full of possibility of loss. When entering a trade, you must find out the whole market trend of the stock seeing its support and resistance and whether it broke any of the two, knowing when to enter and exit that trade. One thing I learn in life from experience it takes the same amount of energy to do the right thing as it does to do the wrong thing. The Jobs that create the most millionaires are doctors, investment banker, lawyer, air traffic control, engineer and financial trader, however, the jobs listed five of these jobs require 7+ years of university, a degree or two, working for someone else/having a boss and a 30 year career to get there, the latter job (financial trading) can be learned at any age, at any time and done from anywhere in the world and can be represented in proportional dimensions based on how you progress in it. A million dollars - $1,000,000, making it in 365 trading days is very easy and not complex, below I have broken it down to the minute on the trading day on the financial Stock market in the United States.

$1,000,000 ÷ 12 months = $83,333.3333 per month

$83,333.3333 ÷ 4 weeks = $20,833.3333 per week

$20,833.3333 ÷ 5 days = $4,166.6666 per day

$4,166.6666 ÷ 6.5 hours = $641.0256 per hour

$641.0256 ÷ 60 minutes = $10.6837 per minute

The United States stock market opens 9:30am Eastern Time Monday to Friday and closes 4:00pm Eastern Time. They do however have after hour trading up to 8:00pm Eastern Time. One million dollars might seem like a lot but broken down to how much to make per minute it doesn't seem like a lot anymore. The U.S Stock Market is worth $30 Trillion dollars. We have to first know why the Stock market exist in the first place, it does so to help with raising capital for companies through the issuance of new and secondary shares and to facilitate the exchange of shares from one owner to another. In the United States equity market, there are over 6 billion trades a day. To get the ball rolling in making a million dollars in 365 days you will need a good broker one with little or no commission and is good for beginners. There are many good brokers out there, E-Trade, TD Ameritrade, Robin-hood etc. Then funding your account, you don't need a lot of money to make money on the stock market you just need to master your emotions and the fundamentals of trading in this book MAKING MILLIONS FROM THOUGHTS TO REALITY will teach you all you need to know. Fundamental trading is a method where a financial trader's center of attention on company-specific events to determine which stock to buy and when to buy it. I think all markets are controlled and influenced cleverly, unfairly, and/or unscrupulously in the short term for precise detailed structural reasons. Trading on fundamentals is more closely associated with buy-and-hold strategy rather than short-term trading. There are four (4) different trading styles Scalping, Day trading, Swing trading and Position trading. In this book MAKING MILLIONS FROM THOUGHTS TO REALITY we will focus on Scalping and Day trading and how to use it to make $4166.66 consistently on a daily basis with proper risk management and proper entry and exit in each trade. Get a notebook and create a journal, inside of when you enter a trade and why and when you exit the trade, learning from history and profiting from your experience in trading. Before going into the week check the markets and see which stocks will have earnings report the week you are going into and begin looking at the charts and predicting if these companies will be making a profit or loss. For example, Apple stock (AAPL) you can look at the company earnings reports and the market structure and know when to trade this stock. Financial trading as a steep learning curve, it is a profession and if you learn quickly, you can generate massive wealth. Financial trading is really a license to print money daily and it's probably the only profession you can print money from, and the United States of America Secret Service won't come looking for you. The best stocks to trade daily are what are called Stocks in Play. Stocks in Play have three characteristics the first one is they trade at a high volume which means they are being bought and sold very quickly, they are trading independently of the market sector which they are a part of and lastly, they have a fundamental catalyst such as earning reports, merger, or a major product release. You must be wondering how do you value a company and see if the shares are priced accordingly know if you should buy it or short sell it, I will share with you a few approaches in how to value a company and thus understanding how to make a good conclusion or resolution reached after consideration on what to do in a major way is the asset based approach, this is done by taking the company's balance sheet and looking at each asset and making a valuation and see if the shares is appropriately valued with the company, the ratio based valuation is essentially saying looking at a similar company from the same sector and look at their price to share earnings ratio or P/E ratio is the relationship between the current price share ratio to the company's earnings per share, this can be used to find out whether a company is overvalued or undervalued.

$$P/E = \frac{\text{SHARE PRICE}}{\text{EARNINGS PER SHARE}}$$

The Discounted Cash Flow (DCF) forecast the earnings and cash flows that will happen in the future of the company, project, security, or asset and then bring them back to the present money at a discounted rate this is done using the concept of the time value money. If you pay less than the DCF value, your rate of return will be higher than the discount rate and vice versa if you pay more than the DCF value your rate will be lower than the discount.

$$DCF = \frac{CF1}{1+r} + \frac{CF2}{1+r} + \frac{CFn}{1+r}$$

Where:

CF = The cash flow for the given year.

CF1 is for year one, CF2 is for year two

CFn is for any additional years

r = The discount rate

Being a Financial trader, the first major rule is live to trade another day, doing so it's good to practice the one percent rule. Never risk more than one percent of your trading account in any given trade this gives you room to make several mistakes and still not ending up blowing your account. Financial trading is the study of psychology between buyers, sellers, and the undecided. The more you take control of your finances, the less money controls you.

Let's start by talking about wicks and why they are important. Wicks show a sign of rejection and a potential reversal. A wick is a sign of exhaustion when buyers and sellers are losing control of the momentum this will give you confidence on where the market is going or will be going. When looking to enter a trade what you should look for is a clear identifying mark of breaking and closing below structure. Remember trading on emotions and impulse is the recipe for disaster. Doing day trading you will hear about VWAP (Volume Weighted Average Price), this provides the trend and value in a stock. Similar to moving average it shows when the price is bullish or bearish.

$$\text{VWAP} = \frac{\text{SUM OF PRICES} \times \text{VOLUME}}{\text{TOTAL VOLUME}}$$

VWAP is really the price multiply by the number of shares traded and divide that number by the total number of shares traded. To calculate the benchmark on let's say a 10-minute candle chart, you need to find the first average the stock traded at the first 10 minute of the day, you will add the high price, low price and the closing price in that period and divide by 3. Then multiply this number by the volume in that period.

AVG PRICE = $\underline{\text{HIGH + LOW + CLOSING PRICE}}$

PV VALUE OF THE STOCK ON OPENEING

$\underline{\text{HIGH + LOW + CLOSING PRICE}}$ × VOLUME IN THAT PERIOD

3

VWAP VALUE = PV VALUE

VOLUME IN THAT PERIOD

To maintain the VWAP value throughout the day while trading continues to add the PV Value from each period to the prior PV Values and divide it by the total volume up to that point in the trading day. Most trading platforms provide this for you but understanding this VWAP value will provide you with the necessary skill for day trading. VWAP value is a single day indicator, and it begins at the opening of each day of trading.

THE NICKEL

In life you always hear it takes money to make money but that is not true. In order to make millions of dollars yo u need financial literacy and this book "MAKING MILLIONS FROM THOUGHTS TO REALITY", is your handbook to financial freedom. This book of financial literacy is an asset if practiced properly, money will be flowing in your pocket daily. Investing in the financial market you get paid daily, it's a real-life ATM you go in everyday and withdraw and have financial freedom. Society teaches you with their traditional path to go to school, get a job, work hard, save your money, get out of debt retire at 65. The problem with this is you sell all your time for a little money.

"MAKING MILLIONS FROM THOUGHTS TO REALITY" is the manual to financial freedom anywhere you are in the world. Remember money is a tool not a goal. Your main goal is to be a good trader using money as your tool, once you become a good trader the money will be the afterthought just flowing in. It cost the US government 5.4 cents to print a one-dollar bill and printing the $100 bill costs 15.4 cents. The rich make money in the world today from speculating, and from producing goods and services all which form the economic activity to create money from/to money.

Financial education and application with these tips, can make you money twenty-four hours a day and seven days a week without a nine to five. This can make a lot more sense than working hard all the time for fake money and all of your time taken. Assets put money in your pocket whether you work or not. Making money is very easy, in this era while money needs to do the work for you. We are in one of the richest countries in the world, the United States of America.

What most people need to do is study money. Money is considered debt and the United States dollar called the world currency, became debt on August 15, 1971, after

President Nixon took it off the gold standard. This date in history will not be forgotten and has an important date in economic history for many generations and decades. Many people will look back on that day (August 15, 1971) and voice their opinion as to how things could have been done differently as it relates to our currency. Money doesn't exist after this, it's all in your mind.

All the problems we see today in the monetary system are a direct result of the decision made on August 15, 1971. We abandoned our treasure, the finance system backed by gold. What gold did was provided financial discipline on government spending. It was not in the hands of everyone. This created Fiat currency (Fiat is a Latin word and it basically means currency being circulated by force) which is currency backed by nothing, but government promises, greed and abuse of power

When they tell you work and get out of debt, it is impossible because debt is money, and the only way out is for the government to tax you. Ask yourself this question, why you would save money when the government can just print money at any time of their choosing. The bank wants you to save money so they can use their fractional reserve banking system (this system also print money out of thin air) which only a fraction of bank deposits is backed by actual cash on hand and available for withdrawal. The principle on which the practice of this activity is based is done to theoretically expand the economy by freeing up capital for lending. So, the bank is creating more debt and profiting billions of dollars.

In reality, the banks run the world, the wealthy run the banking system and the world. Just ask yourself what's the interest rate the bank is paying you on your savings; not even one percent and you're lucky if you get that much. As in inflation is going up, this means your money is losing value. Just look at the price for similar items one, five, ten and twenty years ago. When the bank lends out money, that is how money is created through debt and not through you saving. If you're going to be successful and wealthy in life you have to find the best teachers and these people are on the inside of the rich and wealthy and the people who are running the banks.

In order for the United States economy to function, they have to borrow money from the rest of the world and the more money they loan us today they have to loan more money in the future, if these countries stop loaning us the whole economy will collapse. Credit is a vital part of the banking system and the global economy. The bank made credit to be a more readily available "asset" to more individuals.

The banking system figured that debt and credit helps drive growth, helps companies deploy capital, helps employment support, small businesses and the list goes on and on. You have to decide where your head space is and what is on your mind. Hopefully for your future, should be on creating wealth in the asset column. Everybody can make money and become financially free, but your head space has to be in the right space.

What makes you rich is what's in your head space and what you are thinking. When and if your financial knowledge increases, your money will also increase with direct proportion. It is always good to put money in the game and see what it does. This will also spark your interest about gaining financial freedom. A 401K was made for a retirement as what many people think who are working until sixty-five years.

After the Great Depression in 1929 which lasted 10 years, has sent Wall Street into a panic and wiped-out millions of speculators. After this, people were not getting into the stock market, so they created a 401k to make it easy for the average Jane and Joe to get into the stock market. In today's world you cannot save yourself to retirement because the interest rates the banks are giving is less than 1 percent coupled with inflation or deflation on the dollar. This would not make any sense because you would be in the negative with all the fees you are paying, especially if the Federal Reserve keeps printing money. Ironically, your money will be losing value daily and become worthless as the printing of money from thin air continues with only the government promise backing it; who else can print money? The stockbrokers are really the ones benefiting from the 401k. They get paid fees whether the stock goes up or down on your 401k.

Never turn your money to someone else to manage; nobody will care about your money but you. financial education is the best advice I can give you; you have to get smart with your money. You can start by reading this book "MAKING MILLIONS FROM THOUGHTS TO REALITY" and taking it around with you daily.

This book will guarantee you financial freedom. Start taking classes in taxes and money management. These lifelong skills you will need to become rich and stay rich. Never save money to get out of debt because the Federal

Reserve is just printing money, instead of creating several streams of assets which will generate income.

Assets will always put money in your pocket whether you work or not. Wasting your time, on that job, you can never be paid for your time. Getting a degree and collecting a paycheck every month, are you comfortable putting your life into the governments hand allowing them to dictate your future? This book "MAKING MILLIONS FROM THOUGHTS TO REALITY" is here to elevate the financial well-being of every human being when it is possible.

During all my systematic investigation into my time studying of the materials and resources, I learned that in order to establish facts and reach new conclusions, I have come to the reasoning that successful people always know what they want. The focus should never be on the how you will get anything, but the focus should be what you want, and when I say what you want, it should be what exactly do you want. Take responsibility for your life and whatever you want, and I am talking in regard to all of it. Don't ever buy into the belief system that life is hard, making money is hard, you have to make it a point of order in your mind where everything thing begins.

I believe all the millions begin in your mind first and making your life a living reality, begins in your mind first. Almost eighty percent of Americans are living paycheck to paycheck. This book was designed to take you away from that mentality and you will gain financial freedom. You have to get your mind right before things can happen in reality. I believe the percentage of unhappy people is in direct proportion to the people in America living paycheck to paycheck. In order to escape all of this, we have to unlearn everything we were taught in school about getting a student loan and working hard until sixty-five, in a job and pay taxes. This has been instilled in many of us. So, you must put forth your best efforts to unlearn all what they have taught you in school. Rewire your brain about what is real and what is not real. "MONEY IS NOT REAL STOP WORKING FOR IT"!

As stated, our behaviors are based on our thoughts. Right wired minds deal with knowing what is real from what is fake is the key. You can change and rewire your mind as you keep working on yourself. Your brain is the biggest investment you can make in your lifetime. As you constantly work on yourself, transforming your brain, changing your neurology to change your insights, are crucial also. To change the outside world is not the way to go, you have to change what's inside first so the things that you want will be attracted to you. If you want a good future and you want to predict your future the best way to do it is creating it.

Rewiring your mind and get your mind to create the future that you want, your body is the servant to your mind not the mind the servant to the body. Once you become fully aware of how money works, it gets much more difficult to spend money on stuff like a new car, brand new clothes, and flashy things. It will get much easier to drop money on yourself by continuing to train your mind through education. Educating yourself is vitally important through self-education or classes. Even to trade more stocks, bonds, and derivatives, buy rental properties and several other cash flowing assets that bring in more money to you and in your pocket. You are in control of your life and all that is in it, this means you are in control of your greatest asset, your mind, and you have the power to control it.

Rewire your mind to whatever you want to do, you decide your happiness and you decide how much wealth you want; you have all the power to create your future no matter what happened in your past. You also have the ability today and right now to begin rewiring your mind and creating the future you want. Ameliorate your mind, train your mind to think in abundance and wealth, free yourself from all the psychological slavery.

Rewiring begins with unlearning all the garbage we have been taught in society. We have to lay down authoritatively destructiveness because it is controlling you. Your most valuable asset is your mind and if you even think about it and understand the most valuable things in your life are the things that are priceless and can never be bought. School is made to only develop your intellect, meaning get good grades and getting a job. You don't need intellect to make money, you need knowledge. Remember knowledge is power!

I found out this to be true that school doesn't teach awareness and learning to control your greatest asset, your mind. Your mind without a doubt, is your most valuable asset. You must rewire it and train it to create the future you want. You have to decide your future, no government or no job decides your future, you decide the future you want. No way you should keep repeating the same thing over and over and getting negative results and think things will change. It has nothing to do with what is going on with the outside world. Believe it is nothing about the government, the economy, the president, it all depends on the individual and each individual who wants change.

I can tell you this for a fact, you don't need a financial product, or any "hot stock pick", you need to change your mind set about money. Your future is in your hands, rewriting your thoughts and focus on your happiness and your wealth by writing down exactly want you want and your dreams and goals should scare you. Stress in medical terminology can be defined as any type of change that causes physical, emotional, or psychological strain. External and internal stressors work on the body and respond to anything that requires attention or action. Stress causes changes in the body that leads to raised blood pressure, heart rate and blood sugar levels. It may also cause feelings of fear, envy, jealousy, frustration, depression, anxiety, and anger. All of this means that our thoughts can make us sick. Therefore, if at all possible, your thoughts could make you sick then it is very possible that your thoughts can make you well. If your thoughts can make you well, it can also be wired to make you wealthy and happy. The five is the past, moving forward to the next digit.

At this moment in your life when you start feeling abundant and worthy, you are generating wealth. The moment you're empowered and feeling it, you're commencing the steps towards the success you want in your life. At this moment when you start feeling whole, the rewiring of your mind begins, you will begin to feel real happiness and love, all of life and all you want will be attracted to you; all of life abundance that truly belongs to you.

You see what the Covid 19 Virus has done to the economy. Whether it was caused due to a lab leak in China or due to the bats infecting humans we don't know, but during this economic lockdown and many people losing their jobs and business, the richest 1% in the world got richer. They are no different than you are; they just have rewired their mind. How can you even dream so big, when serving a God so big? Success begins in the mind, and it takes a lot of repetition after you unlearn the negative stigmas you were told early in life to distort your thinking.

I learned that the subconscious mind is simply power without direction, and it does what it is told to do. Every human being has the power within to prosper and live-in abundance. Our God is a God of abundance and prosperity

Nothing in this world stands between all that you want but yourself, doubt, and fear has to flee when you call it out. Did you know when you rewire your mind and dream big, wish without any worrying, all your wishes will be a command, all that you desire will be fulfilled. If you want something worthwhile remember your environment is a mirror of each individual mental attitude.

Actions trigger feelings just as feelings trigger action, life is interesting only to interesting people, same as life is successful only to successful people. Many people in today's society confuse money with wealth and this is thus by far a major problem and why many in society have suffered and is still impoverished.

Money doesn't come from nowhere and it never did, and it never will. Money in reality, exist as an idea, but it never has and never will be of a concrete existence as it relates to quantity. The spoils in life go to the risk takers, the individual who uses all is time to take action and go all in for their goals will achieve those goals.

An individual living on their own must think and rewire their mind to get ahead in the world. The only limit in becoming wealthy is you; all you need is a plan, the will to carry out that plan and a rewired and constantly trained mind. As you train and rewire your mind, remember to keep money in its properly place, it is a servant nothing more. You should keep it in its place and use it for what it is, “a tool”. Never allow money to be nothing more or it will become the master and you the servant. Your affluence in life will be in direct proportion to your service.

The key to the door for every individual on earth to becoming wealthy is in your mind, there is nothing as powerful in human creation, than the mind. I cannot stress this enough over and over until you get it; creating massive wealth is not a hard science, and you do not need an elite degree or certificate. It is really nothing but a common skill and how you conduct yourself towards creating the wealth is more important than what you know.

I cannot stress this enough, disciplining your mind. Giving it a command and then let the body follow it. Form great wealth generating thoughts by rewiring your mind and these will develop in great habits and make them your masters. Therefore, you will have no place for bad habits because all habits are learned, and you can replace the bad broke negative habits with great habits. Habits that are result oriented, by making a list of important things you need to do and discipline yourself to work on these techniques until it is completed.

Begin today by rewiring your mind and start practicing good habits, wealth creating habits that will allow you to reach your goal. Great habits paired with focused thinking, will bring energy and power towards anything that concerns you, be it whether physical or mental. Life was exponentially designed to give us what we deserve. The computer that I am writing this book on right now was first created in the mind of an individual before it was the physical computer. You have to decide exactly what you want and how you want to live; imagine it, create this wealth and this lifestyle in your mind. You will never be wealthy by societies definition of making money where salary = going to a job every day.

If you have a job and the job pays you $25 per hour, and you are working a 40-hour week it will take you over twenty years to make one million dollars and that one million dollars is without taxes and expenses. Now you see the average everyday person working, it would take all there lifetime to do this and the person would have to be living frugally and they will have lost the most valuable thing "TIME". Let me give you some facts and believe me when I tell you many wealthy people don't want you to hear this. I don't care who you are, where you're from or what your background, anyone the regular Jane and Joe can do this. This system is so easy, yet it is real, and many have kept it a secret, but it is not a secret anymore.

Let's face it a school is a business, colleges and universities are huge businesses and the certificates, degree, masters, and doctorate they are telling you to go in debt for it is a consumer product. Some educational institutions are selling you a consumer product at a very expensive price and often times we cannot afford it.

Americans alone owe $1.5 trillion in student loan debt where 44.7 million people carry that student loan debt. I am not smarter than any of you, be the bull in whatever you have going on, fight for the life you want never settle. If you get your mind in tuned with reality, all sorts of illusions and delusions will disappear, you have to stay in the fight. Many people have a distorted mindset in such a serious way that most people would rather have money than real wealth. Take the actions and steps to start priming your main to start achieving the financial goals (a dream with a deadline) you want in your life today. There are no rational restrictions relating to what you can achieve in life other than those restrictions that exist in your mind. What you want and have been is and have been up to you. You the individual are your own limit and don't let anyone tell you otherwise. Take responsibility of your own life.

Never stop learning and working on your mind, train and tame that beast, the most powerful computer. The ability to have a strong rewired mind with persistence make an unbeatable combination for success. Rewiring your mind to generate wealth works with the reality and the energy of the present moment.

Did you know, to manifest millions and real wealth, we must begin from in the mind and then the things we want will be attracted to you. We must develop a healthy relationship with your mind so that everything else around you are aligned to it. A wealth generating mind with a strong intuition will lead to you mastering your mind and thoughts and thus will begin to radiate your thoughts outward in a very intentional way and the world around you will match your thoughts and the things you want.

THE DIME

Often times we want to know what margin trading is and how to use it. In uncomplicated terms, when you make a deposit in your brokerage account, your broker gives you leverage (increased buying power) meaning you will be able to make practical and effective use of more buying power as the brokerage is giving you a loan like what any bank will do to trade.

There are three main subsets of margin trading that you first need to understand before you use it. Day trading (Intraday) margin, Initial (overnight) margin and Maintenance margin. For financial day traders and if that is your main focus, you should consider using day trading (intraday) margin. Real financial education should tell you why money, bitcoin and crypto is going up and down.

In July 1944 there was a negotiated and legally binding arrangement between parties as to a course of action and system called the Bretton Woods. This was negotiated by delegates from forty-four countries. Relating to this accord, gold was the basis for the U.S. dollar and other currencies were aligned to the United States dollar's value. This system came to an end in 1971 when President Richard Nixon took the dollar of the gold standard. Therefore, the volatility in the dollar, bitcoin, gold, and silver was diminished denoting saving money is really for losers.

Saving money now makes no sense as interest rates are at their lowest and inflation at the highest (2021). What this means is your money is losing value. The Federal Reserve Bank, as a matter of fact, can just print money out of thin air, but you also can print your own money, just a different process. Technically, you can create your own money to invest in the stock market and become a millionaire. It is really an accounting stratagem; a tool the banks use to create money. They do not really give out loans to people. When the people borrow borrow money from the bank, the bank makes as is that you have deposited the money to create what is called the liability. This is how the money supply is created.

The first way money is created is through debt by the Federal Reserve Bank; the second way is through equity. Equity in the stock market is the value of the shares issued by a company. In 2019, one Amazon stock was valued $1650and in 2020 one Amazon stock was valued $3200. On the market floor, the asset increased by $1550. Investors who bought Amazon stocks made their equity (Amazon stock) increased in value without doing any physical work. Wealth was created because investors bought an asset and it increased in value. This is breaking news!

There are four assets in life that can make you rich; they have subsets. Ironically, there are four assets in life that make you wealthy, they are business, real estate, stocks, and commodities. Most of the billionaires have business like Amazon, Facebook, Microsoft etc. Commodities are like gold, oil, corn and etc. I have focused on generating wealth through the stock market as it is a proven way of making millions of dollars.

My viewpoint and the viewpoint of other financial experts is that the markets currently are too complacent regarding inflation and if inflation does prove to be higher than expectations. It also can result in higher commodities price (gold, silver) and interest rates. The best indicator of inflation, you can always check the economy and the financial market to see if there is an increase in the money supply.

Our success and failure have nothing to do with the opinions of others. It has only to do with the opinions of ourselves and what we are doing. The only person who can be considered a failure is that person who tries to succeed at nothing. The accomplishment of an aim or a purpose lies in striving, reaching, and attempting. Any person who makes a decision on a goal and step out to launch in achieving the goal, is a success right there. In all walks of life, the most successful people are the risk takers; they take the risk of being novel and unusual.

What I learned through listening to others, any person who takes risk knows that nothing is wrong with failure it is just a learning experience. We find the solution to our own problem by being of service to others. The only difference with the individuals making big money and small money is because, the one trading big money decided to and make it their business to do so. As a trader, you must make a decision to go with your heart; if and when in doubt, look up the rules for making money. We are all self-made but only successful people will admit this.

Knowledge is available to everyone. We have to decide who we want to teach us; whether the experts who are generating wealth or broke people who keep complaining daily. The key to every individual success lies in your mind and the magnificent and priceless cerebrum behind your eyes and between your ears. It is all the gold mine you need, everything you need is there and begins there.

Your total surroundings and conditions for any adult in which they live and operate is a reflection of you as a person to include our job, the house, the car you drive and all the people you are involved with on a regular basis. If you feel your total surroundings and conditions for any adult in which you live and operate can change, you have only to ameliorate your mind and your world will moderately change. Historically noted, as a man soweth, so he shall reap and whatever he continues to reap so shall he soweth in hope that your sowing is bountifully. You should always remember we become what we think about most of the time and whatever we continue to think about that's how we will remain. You can have all you want in this world; you only need to make up your mind. I cannot say this enough! He who works with the wise will be wise. Your perspective will change once you are around people who are making one million a month.

The universe plays no favorites. It is impersonal towards every individual. If we don't like what's going on in our environment, then we must change it and the change begins in your mind. Actions trigger feelings just as feelings trigger actions. There is nothing at all to be gained from being negative so why not just be positive. I learned to think positive, think, and act like I am wealthy and worked towards it and it until it has happened. Success or failure is all caused by your mental attitude. As you rewire your mind to become wealthy and successful, everything will fall into place. The most auspicious people in the world are those who know where to place value appropriately.

Whatever you are looking for must be found within yourself, it must be found first within you, whether it is success, wealth, or riches. Everything we do outwardly is only an expression of what we are internally, what exist in the mind. You will always become what you think about, and any ideas formed are worthless unless you work on them. I Cannot stress this enough!

As in the scriptures, ask and it shall be given; seek, and ye shall find, knock and it shall be opened unto you: The only people who make money are those who work in a mint. The rest of us have to earn money and before we do so, we must understand how to rewire our mind, to have a wealth mindset. As many would think success is not the result of making money instead making money is the result of success. Also, many have this thought that you are successful if you make a lot of money. In truth and reality, it is the other way around; you have to be successful first before you make money.

There are many things in this world that exist that we don't see because we are not looking for them or capable of looking for them. the world we see is the world we look for. For example, different people looking outside an airplane window after taking off and hovering over the city. Some will see things from a different viewpoint; one will say this is a rundown torn up city and one might say what a stunning opportunity for real estate and another has his face buried in his phone and their interest is different and will see nothing.

Allow me to reiterate this again, the only person who can be called a failure is the person who tries to succeed at nothing. Failure consists of not trying and not striving. Your success lies in reaching and attempting any course or action, when someone decides to carry out their goals and is not based on the opinions of others, but it is for his or her personal success. Anyone who adds to their prosperity will be prosperous in turn.

As I went through my journey in reaching success, I noticed that the successful people are the risk takers, moving towards their own goals, standing up for what is right. I saw they reckoned with, there is nothing wrong with failure; they picked up themselves and stayed the course

Albert Einstein proved that all the energy of the universe is constant and that it can neither be created or destroyed. He noted, it can only be converted from one form to another, Therefore, energy cannot be created in any individual but understand that it is there, and it only needs to be activated, and most your dreams will be fulfilled. The human being who knows what he wants, knows the need to study for his or her directions in order to achieve their goal.

This book does not cost much, but you can generate ideas from reading it, it can bring you more value than you have now. The useful value will greatly exceed its cost by separating the facts from the opinions and analyze the facts to include information shared. I have learned, learning is never done, and your thinking should never cease. These two must be continued throughout your lifetime to impart purpose and direction in your life. You have all that you need to live, the key is giving more than you want to receive, the debt will be owed to you.

It is without a doubt, as we relentlessly give more, love, respect, creating instead of competing this would bring out the fire in you and the fire in you will ignite that creativity that lies in you, and you will learn that you are the creative center of your universe. All increase must come from you personally, from internal and your outward environment will reflect on what you are doing internally. I did not realize this was so powerful until I begin to unleash me through giving and respecting.

Imagination is the key to motivating yourself. Everything will begin to fall in place and your life will bring far greater rewards. Everything we see about us in the present was once an invisible idea that was formulated in the mind of a human being. We become what we think about and to develop ideas, a person has to question everything and lead an active inquiring mind; we should be discreet about it. We live in a changing world and changes for the better is always good.

I am learning more and more that one of the reasons we are here on earth is to serve human beings and to the extent we serve our fellow human beings will help us determine our reward in life. The universal key to success is as you think so shall you become, it has never changed as in the scriptures so as a man thinketh, so shall he become. My take of this is as he continues to think, so he will remain. As the word states, therefore all things whatsoever ye that men would do to you, do ye even so to them: for this is the law and of the prophets.

As a financial day trader, I am always trying to leverage the stock market as much in my favor, as possible. As you developed a financial trading plan, think of as a pyramid where you have a strong base to begin with a long-lasting strong foundation. Think out of the box! This will elevate your thoughts as you to move to the top of the pyramid.

A trading plan tilts the odds in your favor. As a financial trader, the SPY is an ETF, and it tells you what's going on in the market daily. If you see a stock and it is above the SPY, you know that stock is doing good for that day. In say that, this is a stock you want to go bullish on. If a stock is below the SPY, you would want to go bearish on that stock. You might want to sell it because it is weak compared to what's going on in the market. There is always a gray area but putting everything into context this is a way to short and long stocks, by putting all the odds and probabilities in your favor.

The Higher the ego, the more the mistakes. Ego is a wealth destroyer. The Higher the patience, the better the outcome. Patience is a wealth creator and when we get above that nickel, we know we are on the way to bigger and better. Let's take everything step by step after checking in with your broker and have funded your account. Educate yourself first by using paper trading. This is when you trade using fake money until you get a hang off it, then you start trading with your funded account.

On a daily basis, you always hear about stocks that run 100%, 300%, 700% in a day, I will be showing you what stocks to basically look for daily. Also, this will show you where all the stocks are being traded and the volume is to keep your eye on. In during that, day you can make a lot of money off them. Before the market open, you scan for stocks that are "gapping up". "Gapping up", really means stocks that are moving up in price. Before the stock market opens, you need to scan to see which stock is being traded the most by the traders.

You can use the E Trade, TD Ameritrade Think or Swim, FINVIZ or other platforms to scan for which stock is up the most % or down the most percent % to day trade. Traders trade the stocks with the most volume and that could result in the best news of that day. If the stock is gapping up and there is no good news, most likely, you will not want to trade that stock. If the stock has good news and the stock is going up its good to trade because there is a strong possibility the stock is going up that day.

Winning stocks have certain characteristics that you have to look for, so as to profit daily. They are stocks that have high volatility. Analysts like these stocks and see them being profitable with positive previous earnings and have high target prices.

Support and resistance are popular terms used in trading and are terms for two levels on a price chart that appear to limit the market's range of movement. The support level is where the price regularly stops falling and bounces back up, while the resistance level is where the price normally stops rising and dips back down. Support and Resistance areas are regularly broken. They work on all time frames whether one minute, one day one week etc.

One of the main things not to do is get emotionally

unattached to money this is the best advice I can give you. You want to be trading on the charts in front of you not on any emotions. Nobody is perfect but if you are following my advice and using data and trading with the proper techniques, you will become a profitable financial trader. Investing in stocks you care about is very important but not always profitable for you. For example, if you really like apple products you will give a lot of thought into it. Especially following their news and earnings and products they are launching. I know I told you not to have any emotional attachment with money, however there is nothing wrong with having an emotional attachment to a stock or product you care about. Researching that company and follow what's going on with that company or industry. Always try to buy stocks on sale. Buying low and selling high, that's exactly how you make a profit.

My center of interest and activity is to trade in the morning from 9:30 am EST to 10:30am EST; that's when we have the most buyers and sellers on the market and the most volume and volatility. Therefore, it is easy to get in and out of a trade with a profit fast. As a financial day trader, it is always a matter of importance to search for volatility and volume and be a very quick thinker to get in and out of these trades thinking about your risk tolerance and your rewards ratio. Every trader needs a trading plan that gives you an edge. You don't have to profit in all your trades, you can be wrong thirty percent of the time with proper risk management, and you make a profit. Remember we don't have to be right hundred percent of the time.

We are trading against computers that are algorithms. Computer's algorithms are moving around sixty percent of shares daily, running the price up and down. News is very important in trading every day, I look for the news every day to see what will drive the particular stocks up or down in that day. Get in the breakout, get your profit, and come off the market. I trade real stocks. I don't trade penny stocks or FOREX.

I avoid pre-market trading because the volume is usually low. If you don't mind trading a couple of shares, you can do pre-market trading. There is an easy way to find stocks to trade daily using stock scanners. This software scans the markets for you," www.trade-ideas.com" which is a very good scanner. Always track your trades and see what you are good at in every trade. You may take a note of it because this will give you a very good idea of what you are good at.

As a beginner trader, there are tools which will assist you in trading, these are free tools that will benefit you and your trading plan. Investopedia is where you can get explanations for terms you see in the SEC filings which will explain free terms. This website you can look up SEC filings of stocks.

We Bull is a free trading commission app, it is very good to practice paper trading (the simulated trading of buying and selling financial instruments without using real money), you get live data trading for free, you also get a good stock pre-market scanner. Your trading goal should not be profit related, what you should you focus on is mastering your strategy, as a trader your goal is to be a good trader, the profit will come afterwards. No strategy or trading style is perfect or full proof because the market is always trading adapting and quick thinking are necessary on the market. Creating a watch list is very important for volatile stocks and stocks with good price actions, stay up to date with news and market sectors. I will be sharing my stock list that I watch daily and that I mostly trade, I look at news in the morning and see if there is a catalyst to move the stock. I trade Tech stocks that move the market, APPLE, AMAZON, GOOGLE, TESLA etc. Confirmation, direction, and position sizing are very important in a trading day. Treat support and resistance as Zones not exact prices, buy at support Sell at resistance. The more times a stock touches a price level the more valid the support and resistance level is. Successful traders should ensure risk is their main focus not reward, losing does not feel good because nobody likes to lose money, trading is not how much money you make trading but how much you don't lose.

Winning trades are only good if they are bigger than your losing trades, your risk comes first not the reward. The market as no rules or boundaries, it's impossible to predict the market with guaranteed certainty. Only 12% of millionaires inherited wealth the rest built it from the ground up. The most obsolete idea in this world today is go to school get a job, get a paycheck, and pay back your student loan. Work until 65 or maybe more to retire then live for 10 years if you are lucky so work all your life to enjoy 10 years of retirement. Never exchange your time for money let your money work for you. Getting a paycheck is the biggest obstacle in your life and that is what 99% of the people are doing today selling their time for money by getting a paycheck. If you work for money, you are taxed a lot. When you have the money work for you pay little to no tax.

Education is good but it could be obsolete because too many people are doing it. You must get in the entrepreneurship mindset developing ideas and business that the market needs. No economy is bad there is always an opportunity in every economy on every market. Saving money or working for money is the biggest scam, the United States Mint is printing money every day, so why save or work when they are just printing? There are three kinds of income earned income is for employees, capital income is for capital gains like buying and selling stocks and cash flow income. Remember use debt as money because the bank is printing it every day.

Money is created through debt, but people have to understand the tax code of their country never say you can't always ask yourself HOW CAN I AFFORD IT. The Bible say words become flesh; you do not need money to make any money. To be rich and successful, debt is a useful tool in getting there. You have to train your mind, that's the beginning of everything, never follow the crowd, to get in the mindset that live below your means and scrum to become rich, that's the furthest thing from the truth, this is a total annihilation to your spirit. The truth is you have to know good investment from bad investment because it all boils down to your financial intelligence.

In the United States since 2008, America's national debt has surged nearly two hundred percent, reaching $27 trillion as of October 2020. Short selling is a very simple concept, a trader borrows a stock, sells the stock, and then buys the stock again to return it to the lender. A Short seller is betting that the stock they sell will drop in price, the dissimilarity between the sell price and the buy price is the profit. It is very important to keep away from stocks that are being heavily traded by institutions instead trade stocks that other retail traders are trading. The stocks that are gapping up and down are the stocks financial day traders will be trading, also it is good to be in a community of traders like a chatroom so you will know where they will be trading. I trade mostly only between 9:30 ET and 10:30ET that time is when the most volume is on the market.

Lunch trading hours and evening trading hours are very risky as many traders who I consider amateurs trade at this time. They have lost money in the morning and are trying to get back the money at this time. I try to hit my daily goal at 10:30ET. Once I get that money, I stay back unless I see a trade in the lunch hours or evening trading session. The main aim of a trader is trading the right stocks daily, stocks that have a catalyst.

To day trade, you will need at least $25,000 in your account and most trading platforms will leverage you four stars, if you have the $25,000 and you will be giving a $100,000 to trade daily. If a trader makes four or more-day trades in a rolling five business day period, the account will be labeled immediately, as a pattern day trade account. Certain limitations will then be applied based on the account equity. Account equity is the amount of cash that would exist if every position in the account was closed, this is sometimes called the liquidation value.

The requirement is to maintain a minimum account equity of $25,000 if the trader can. The trader may trade as frequently as desired, however if you trade more than three times in a day trade without maintaining the minimum balance, the account will become restricted from day trading and all positions must be held overnight. When trading, I always trade in sevens, meaning when I am buying stocks, I buy 7, 70, 700, 7000 etc.

The number seven is one of the most significant number

in the Bible and it has some significance in all major religions. Many scholars say it denotes completeness or perfection. After creating the world, Jehovah rested on the seventh day and the seven-day week has been adopted by all human societies. Financial day trading can have you living a lavish lifestyle making thousands of dollars a day; this is a lucrative business for investors. It takes time to get good at it, but the payoff is worth it. You do not need a high IQ to trade, you need a stable personality. Trading is a business where you think, and your facts and reasoning are right.

You make money when buying a stock, not selling the stock. This means when you buy the stock its way below its value and when you buy, you're already in profit making your money on your way in, not out. Always remember price is not equal to value… when looking at a stock, that price has nothing to do with the intrinsic value; usually you the see the stock price fluctuating. This is a representation of supply and demand not the actual value of the company fluctuating.

You must learn to ignore Wall Street noise when trading if you are trading every day. It is beneficial to Wall Street in terms of commissions. These short-term opinions are pushing you to buy and sell without not knowing what you are doing, especially in your early stages of trading. All this is, just noise learn to ignore. Invest based on value while being patient, trading takes time, but it is a very lucrative business. Investing is a marathon not a one-hundred-meter sprint. All the small trades and profits do is add up at the end of the year.

I avoid trend lines, because they are wishful thinking the market only care about price levels, which this takes you on your way to the big quarter. This is where horizontal support and resistance makes sense, because when a downtrend hit support, the market hit backs so fast like a ball hitting a ground. The same way it hits the resistance and bounces back, traders buy and sell in these areas.

To find high probability breakout trades, you want to find the stock that within the last six to twelve months have moved the most in that period. You really want to avoid trades when the market is doing power moves. Most likely, institutions moving the market are huge and fast and its prone to big reversals. The market moves too fast too soon, and you don't want to be chasing the market. In trading always remember for someone to profit someone must lose. Look for a buy opportunity after a strong pull back in the market avoid shorting stocks.

Trading individual stocks on the stock market offers more trading opportunities. I do not hold options overnight or over the weekend due to the volatile market. As one news can change the value of your stock to nothing. It's always good to look left on the chart to see the full support and resistance and also to see previous support and resistance. A consolidation has two ways it can be broken when it breaks and start a new uptrend. This is a very good time to go long on a trade or when it starts a new down trend. This could be unlimited quarters coming your way!

THE QUARTER

Many people have asked me what it takes to be a profitable financial trader. Your trading system has to have a positive expectancy, a statistical edge over the market and you need a specific set of entries and exit rules in each trade. In a trading system, you either exit with a stop loss or loss. Risk is a fixed percentage of your capital for every trade, but your risk is always one to three, so you are risking one percent of your capital to make three percent or more.

For many people money is an emotional thing; most times when you are in a trade, and you see your money go up and down you get emotional and forget your plan. Eighty percent of trading on the market is analyzing twenty percent is trading. The highest probability is trading stocks on an uptrend and entering the retracement when the price drops and hit a level of support.

First of all, you have to remember nobody can predict the future or nobody can predict the market; only gamblers think they can do that and eventually they will lose everything. Some of our multi-billionaires we think is a financial trading professional, cannot predict the market.

Always remember when entering a trade to wait for the confirmation. Remember as a trader you never trade on prediction but trade on confirmation. To be a successful trader, what many books or person won't tell you strategy is only ten to fifteen percent, psychology is fifty to seventy percent, while strategy is only twenty to thirty. Analyzing the market with no emotions is always the best way to trade. You will be able to make proper decisions as I always say, "it is always good to start a paper trading account". You can use E Trade or TD Ameritrade and learn how to develop your trading strategy. Therefore, since it is not real money, you will be trading with less emotions; noting like being stable as you trade.

Trading is a statistical game you earn off probability. You won't win all your trades but if you cut your losses fast and your wins are big, you will be profitable. There are basically three strategies to earn money. Trade your time for money which is risky because most people run out of time. Investing money to let it grow usually through investors with a good track record. Lastly, investing money to make money, making the money that works for you. The best time to invest is NOW when everyone thinks it's risky.

The best stocks to day trade are called stocks in play. There are specific things to look for when initiating day trading. Being a day trader you're as good as the stocks you are trading. Financial day trading is the study of mass psychology, you have to pick the winners between the buyers, sellers and indecisive. Learning how to risk manage is not the hardest part of trading but it is important. You don't need to be a genius or have a high IQ to trade and profit. You have to look for stocks that are trading in a high volume. This makes buying and selling easy.

Stocks with a fundamental catalyst like earnings report such as Merger and the like, are trading independently of the market, meaning that similar stocks aren't moving like those. If you want to reap the long rewards of trading, you have to stay trading and not blow your account. With education and the proper work ethics, this can put you in profit very easily. Most people have ideas and can generate these ideas but the challenge many people have is monetizing the ideas. Remember, in trading consistency is key. You want to always stick to your trading strategy and never forget, discipline is key entering and exiting a trade.

Preservation of capital is key when you get out at the wrong time; you can always make it up again. You need to focus on your risk management and the percentage and quality of your trade, while sticking to your trading strategies. In all that's said and done, you need to master the learning curve and the market; what are the ins and out of the market.

One of the main things a trader as to get right is the "HIT RATE". This is the number of times you are right in a trade. If you can maintain a high "HIT RATE", you will be a successful trader. The number one reason people don't get what they want is because they are not sure as to what they want. In order to make a million of dollars or more in your lifetime, it takes a lot of analyzing and hard work, but it is possible. Failure is not an option. I am committed in making millions of dollars and becoming wealthy, I will die trying. This takes focus, knowledge, expertise, hard work and a rich mindset.

You have to be fully committed to "MAKING MILLIONS FROM THOUGHTS TO REALITY for the average person, in order to make it. This has to be important to the individual reading this book, you have to say to yourself" I will be MAKING MILLIONS FROM MY THOUGHTS TO REALITY", on the financial market. You have to make that commitment to yourself, with a plan for it to happen.

I wrote this book because I wanted the regular person to know it is possible for you to be wealthy and successful. I did so myself and I know many others who have done well. It is without doubt, you are able to be successful by gaining the acquired knowledge and skills. I personally, came from rags to riches. Never be embarrassed about being successful; own it, wear it, be proud of being a successful financial trader as you become a multi-millionaire.

The right time to buy a stock is when you have a high probability level of reversal. Buying at a strong support level and at candlestick price action reversal pattern is a bullish pin bar, buying at in oversold situations. Divergence patterns are useful in determining if a trend is going to reverse or continue its course. A divergence takes place when there is a conflict between the price trend and the indicator trend. A bearish divergence trade is valid when a bearish confirmation candle closes below the low of the swing high candle. A bullish divergence trade is valid when a bullish confirmation candle closes above high of the swing low candle.

To make some easy money monthly without trading to add to your portfolio is pretty easy from dividends. Continue reading below as I share with you high yielding stocks that I traded after making significant amounts of money on the market. These have a rate of high return through dividends as you buy and hold these stocks and get dividends payment monthly. They are Shell Midstream (SHLX) dividend yield is 18.04%, Icahn Enterprises (IEP) dividend yield is 15.6%, Chimera (CIM) dividend yield 15.17%, Energy Transfer LP (ET) dividend yield 15.74%.

These shares once purchased using money you have generated from trading. They will just pay you while you do nothing. This is passive income letting your money work for you. How good is that? These are just some of the shares with high dividends yielded. There are many others, and you should do your research and see what you are comfortable trading. Financial day trading requires you to make quick decisions and have a lot of discipline in the market.

Many new traders initially lack the ability to make decisions and maintain composure while under the stress of losing a position. The skill and discipline in day trading are like muscles that require exercise; to grow on the market and making good trades. The talent, skill, and proficiency to make quick decisions in trading and follow your trading rules will improve your experience in trading.

On a day-to-day trading as I stated repeatably, learning to be patient is very important to be a long term successful as a day trader. Always remember ninety percent of trading is analyzing the market. In this market over sixty percent of the volume in the market is Algorithmic trading. This is when computers moving stocks around on a daily basis. As you know, you can't beat a computer. The only way to beat these computers are the ones with a catalyst and volume. Therefore, when a traders beat the algorithms having a high retail interest, it gives retail interest is some type of new catalyst. Stocks will generally trade with the overall trend in the market, unless there is a reason for them not to move that way; you have to be aware of those variables. A penny stock is any stock that trade under five dollars. These stocks are usually considered high-risk investments due to their low price, lack of liquidity, small market capitalization and wide bid ask spread.

Again, divergence patterns are useful in determining if a trend is going to reverse or continue its course. Basically, when we see the price of the stock making higher highs and lower highs, it's a divergence and it's an indication that the price will reverse the same with lower highs and lower lows. A divergence takes place when there is a conflict between the price and the indicator trend. Confluence in trading is when different technical signals come together and anticipate the same price action movement. When all signals say the same thing, whether support and or resistance, candlesticks, or trend lines, the price will go up.

A trend in price is statistically and more likely to continue in the directions of the trend than reverse. Short selling is the process of selling an asset that you do not own at a high price; in the expectation of buying, it back at a lower price. You must be asking how you do this? Your broker borrows the shares on your behalf from other investors who lend their shares out. You then sell the borrowed shares, generating profits under all market conditions whether in uptrends or downtrends, bear, or bullish market; if we have a recession, you still can make money. Shorting stocks exposes you to unlimited risks of loss, while in theory, stocks can increase in price indefinitely but in real market trading it never happens.

THE DOLLAR BILL

This book will give you all the enigma you need to know and how to begin unlocking the wealth generating potential and becoming the successful person you were destined to be. The financial market has made massive wealth for an unsurmountable amount of people; it made them extremely wealthy. These steps have been put to the test by countless individuals and if properly taught and understood it can bring in mountains of wealth for you.

The blueprint I am referring to is what I have mentioned on several occasions, throughout the book. Many of you may not know that the gold is in your possession already. All those who are searching and are ready to gain this vast wealth of knowledge need not look any further, you have just found it.

All wealthy and successful people in the world today have found this treasure and have used it to generate massive wealth. Success comes before making money; money is just the result of being successful. Reading this book of knowledge and facts, MAKING MILLIONS FROM THOUGHTS TO REALITY. will give you the foundation to begin and the groundwork to build. It is for beginners seeking an understanding of the financial market and also how the economy works. It also entails how money really works and how to work to create assets which will pay you.

Schools whether college or universities never tell you about money and what success is really about. Success is really the progressive realization of a dignitary ideal. We become what we think. Historically, whatever you think about that's who you are. You can decide who, what, how and where and when about your life endeavors. You must begin by doing what is of most importance and that is generating your thoughts. Thinking is up to you, the individual.

Ideas are the greatest things on earth, they are the things that change our minds. The future represents great prospects for the individuals who have positive thoughts and ideas and who work towards their goals. Survival should never be the only option for human beings it is of utmost importance as we enjoy our time on earth. When someone succeeds everyone benefits, your family, friends, the community, and it goes on and on.

CRYPTO CURRENCY

Many people might ask what is crypto? Crypto means data encryption. Most people might have only heard of bitcoin. Crypto currency is a digital or virtual currency that is secured by cryptography in which transactions are verified and recorded; maintained by a decentralized system based on block chain technology (a distributed ledger enforced by disparate network of computers). Using cryptography which makes it nearly impossible to counterfeit or double-spend, rather than by a centralized authority. Crypto is seen by most, as the most convenient era ever. Crypto is the transfer of digital assets. Cryptocurrencies have the greatest potential to put banks out of business because of their very nature.

The supply of money in an economy is very elastic and is dependent up on the central banks like the federal reserves. There are many cryptocurrencies. Some have high value blockchain and others have low value blockchain. Types of cryptocurrencies include currency tokens, DeFi tokens, exchange tokens, NFTs, protocol token Privacy tokens, Stock tokens and Utility tokens. There are several trading platforms for cryptocurrency choose the one which best fits you the individual.

Ethereum is a very good cryptocurrency to hold long term in today's world. Billions of people can't open bank accounts, others have their payments blocked. Ethereum's decentralized finance (DeFi) system never sleeps or discriminates. With just an internet connection, you can send, receive, borrow, earn interest, and even stream funds anywhere in the world. The reality now is that most money nowadays is electronic, it's your visa or debit card number in the computer systems. Wow! The money being moved around on a data base. Getting there??

Crypto will continue to climb until the United States government decides to create its own digital dollar. as you can see China is working on creating the digital Yuan as with other countries including EU and the United States. China's digital Yuan is not based on blockchain but work similar to its very commercial existing systems like Alipay;

where users download digital wallets on their phones, where they can save their money. Many people are asking if cryptocurrency is the new digital gold. It is yet to be figured definitively if it is. The fundamental reason why cryptocurrency has value is because people decide it has value and are buying it. Therefore, the valuation of it is, the bottom line is the future of currency is digital whether we like it or not. It is very good to now get a hand in it and learn about the fundamentals and how to trade cryptocurrency. I am all on board!!

COMMODITIES

The commodity markets have seen a surge in investment in recent years; particularly gold which has hit record highs. Commodities are a part of our everyday lives; many may not know that the most valuable commodity of all is information. You may ask what is a commodity?

Traditional commodities are the raw materials we put into other products we use in practically every area of our lives without a second thought. The more traditional commodities fit broadly into areas of agriculture, livestock, precious metals, and energy. A commodity is a raw material or primary agricultural product that has full or substantial fungibility. They can be traded, bought, or sold such as gold, platinum, silver, crude oil, soybean, corn, and livestock. Some commodities are perishable, and some are non-perishable.

Gold and silver are non-perishable meaning you can store it at your house or in a bank vault which is more secure, and it won't go bad. Gold is usually quoted in US dollars and traditionally been used as a hedge to inflation and a classic safe haven for people especially when the stock market is plunging, gold is most popular in making jewelry, but it is used also in electronic devices such as cellphones, laptops and in the aerospace industry as a lubricant. But a non-perishable commodity (especially of food) is likely to decay or go bad quickly especially if not stored properly.

Crude oil is dependent on several factors and these factors determines its volatility, these are global demand, OPEC, political instability, natural disasters, and others. Crops and livestock are significantly affected by the weather if they have diseases, storms or droughts can cause significant problems with the crops and livestock commodities. Politics also play a very important role as well, as some crops are grown more abundantly in different areas of the world. For example, Brazil is the world's largest coffee producer and produces around twenty five percent of the world's supply of coffee. They are consistently making profits from commodities trading. This is not about finding some magical way like, pulling a rabbit out of a hat to discover profitable trades.

Commodities prices have been rising because of increase in demand. Scarcity is often attached when the supply is in demand and whether in high use of metals in emerging countries or on the food side. There has been a growing demand because of more people eating more food and having the wealth to import more food with a variation of the diet which increases the demand for livestock. On the other hand, a reduction in supply of oil because a shortage and mass consumption of oil.

There is no new discovery of oil, and it is being difficult to exploit industrial metals and even agriculture. There is a growing shortage of arable land around the world to supply this new demand and these fundamental reasons are causing commodities price to go up and will continue going up. Commodities will always be volatile and should always be a part of your portfolio.

If inflation is increasing the best way to hedge against

the increasing inflation is investing in real assets such as commodities. Understanding price movements in commodities between demand and supply and the time to get new supply. If the commodities price is suppressed for a long time usually there will be a huge price spike in the future. Silver is now being suppressed in price and will spike in the near future.

The other historical reason to invest in commodities is because of their diversification benefits in a multi-asset portfolio. Commodities investment can be used in tactical ideas, providing investors have a durable view on the oil market. They may take an investment in oil, they may investment in platinum if and when they are interested in a hedge risk type of product. But in the new commodities market, platinum and palladium will be the new lithium of the renewable and green energy market.

I strongly believe that the key to making good investments is buying low. Many investors are finding actual value in this market segment, especially in the commodities market segment where they are most predominant. I truly believe it is very crucial to dwell on the glaring performance discrepancy of the commodities from the previous years until now, by carefully analyzing the charts.

There are two investment trends with regards to commodities. Many will say it is best to invest in the commodities themselves and on the other hand, others say, the mines that extract the raw materials from the earth, directly investing in the company itself. We are living through times in which the world's major central banks have adopted decisions without precedent with regard to monetary principles adopted by the government.

Many experts have said that there has actually already been a high asset inflation with commodities, in principle the obvious protection to monetary disturbances and at this time in the economy, they are lagging behind. In my opinion, it is very odd that we are invested in real assets and believe that the risk of a significant acceleration of inflation cannot be taken for granted and we are well protected with these investments.

Times are getting tougher for the poorer class; many will say we are living in tough times. The entire global economy is on a downturn, and we must do what we can to save our money as early as possible. Commodities trading done right, can generate very strong returns and add what most people want, diversification to our portfolio. Investing in commodities require more specialized knowledge and may carry more risk than more well-known investments. Trading commodities is one of the oldest forms of investment types, dating back centuries. Even today commodities offer a high profit potential because of the steady and increasing global stipulation; this is an ongoing gesture, so be aware. Commodities are certainly not immune to market fluctuations and volatility, but they can still be a great opportunity for a diversified portfolio.

FUTURES TRADING

You may ask what the futures market is, where many may have heard of the most famous of them all. It all started within the Chicago Mercantile Exchange (CME). In my opinion, just the words alone future you know they are talking of time regarded as still to come. A future market/ trading is an auction market in which participants buy and sell commodities and future contracts for delivery on a specified future date at an agreed price between the buyer and the seller. This is real-time business friends!

Futures are exchange traded derivatives contracts that lock in future delivery of a commodity or security at a price set today. Like many derivative products, futures can be confusing when you're trying to understand how changes in the underlying security affect changes in futures prices which affect changes in your margin of trading.

When you buy a stock, you instantly own that stock for the price you paid, however when you buy a futures contract, you're buying an agreement that states you will buy or sell assets at a certain price at a certain time in the future. Trading futures is speculative and is not suitable for all investors. When trading futures, there are several economic reports to consider including Nonfarm Payrolls, GDP, Housing Data, Treasury auctions, Consumer Price Index (CPI), Producer Price Index etc.

The strategies of hedging are the pillars of the futures market also known as a physical settlement. One main use of a futures contract is to allow a business or an individual the opportunity to navigate risk and uncertainty to lock in a fixed price to buy or sell at a future date. Therefore, doing this lessens the risk of having a price change.

Let's look at this in terms of business and the cattle industry. If the price for beef goes up it is good for restaurants but bad for cattle farmers. If the price goes up for beef it is vice versa. The tables turn with livestock futures both cattle farmers and cattle users are able to lock in prices ahead of time. Let us assume two traders agree to $1 for 10 pounds of coffee on a futures contract. If the price of coffee moves up to $1.10, the buyer on the contract makes $0.10 per pound on the coffee. The seller on the other hand loses out on a better deal.

The vast majority of people taking part in the futures market trading are not producers and manufacturers instead they are speculators (investors and traders). There are two futures market investors and traders can choose from the commodity futures which includes agriculture (corn, coffee, cotton, soybean, sugar, wheat, rice), energy (oil, jet fuel, gasoline, natural gas) precious metals (gold, silver, platinum) livestock (cattle, pork belly, hogs).

Financial futures which include Forex (different currency exchange rates), Indices (contracts attached to the Dow Jones, Nasdaq, and S&P 500) Interest rates and Treasuries (contracts revolving around debt). You must be asking how investors and traders make money in the futures market. Well, it takes place from the change in the value of the futures contract itself. This allows investors and traders to make or lose money from the contract and all of this takes place on the futures exchange.

When trading futures, there are two prices you need to pay attention to: the futures price of the specific contract and the spot price (the current of the commodity). There are two ways to make money on a futures trade long position where the value of the contract increases and a short selling position, where the value of the contract decreases. Although the most traded futures contract is the S&P 500 E- Mini and it may change in the future.

At this point in time, it is and how do you know what's the most traded futures. You should check on the open interest and the number amount and you will find the total amount of contracts that is open on that particular future. The futures market is measured for each point and is called a tick. Therefore, the unit of measurement in the futures market is a tick and functions with distance and worth. All ticks are different depending on the type of futures contract therefore all points will be different.

A second use of futures contract allow investors and traders to speculate on the price movement on commodities, currencies, stock market indices and other assets. Futures markets are open virtually 24 hours a day 6 days per week however each product has its own trading hours. Each commodity or financial instrument has a standardized contract size that never changes. For example, one contract of gold futures always represents 100 Troy ounces of gold. Contracts are either financially settled or physically settled when they reach expiry; not always settled financially.

Crude oil futures are not only a very active market to trade but is also one of the most popular instruments available to trade daily. Crude oil is a wonderful opportunity for traders to make standalone income, in the market. Futures were invented for institutional buyers because they have massive spending capital. These dealers were meant to take the actual physical possession of the commodities like barrels of oil or troy ounces of gold. Establishing a price in advance makes the businesses on both sides of the contract, less vulnerable to fluctuations in prices.

BONDS

Bonds are a very common investment tool. However, to many individuals, it is a common mystery because we most likely hear about them on the news, but it is never explained in full as to how they work. A bond is really an IOU and details who owes what, and when debt repayment will be made. Unlike stocks a bond ownership doesn't mean owning part of a company. It simply means an investor is owed a specific sum, which will be paid back at a promised time. One way to protect yourself from a market crash is by holding some bonds in your market portfolio. A bond is simply a loan given to a company or the government by an investor.

When issuing a bond, a company or government borrows money from investor who in turned, paid interest (coupon) on the money they are loaned. Most investors use bonds in hopes of preserving the money they have while gaining additional income. When a company or the government have a project to do, and they need money to do it, they often issue bonds to get capital to pay for the project. The investor gets paid regular interest payments at a certain rate until the bond is matured, they receive back their principal.

Bonds are asset classes and the one of the most necessary vehicles in the financial market; bonds are scrutinized loans. Bonds are very much stable and referred to as a fixed income instrument. Their payments to holders don't fluctuate over time like the value of stocks or dividends payout. Bond prices for the most part, inversely correlate with interest rates (coupon rates). Since a low interest rate usually means the borrower is trustworthy, more people will want to own that bond because there's little risk. On the other hand, high interest rate reduces from evidence and reasoning rather from explicit statements which is a risky borrower. This can increase the chances a bond becoming worthless, therefore making them cheaper.

There are four things to look at when purchasing a bond: interest rate (coupon rate), coupon period, maturity date and the face value. A bond rating reflects the defaults risk of the company or the government issuing that bond. The default risk is the risk that a bond issuer may be unable to make payments when they become due. The higher the default risk, the lower the rating of a bond and vice versa. A lower rating means lenders will demand a higher interest rate (coupon rate) before providing money.

For investors, a higher rating means a safer investment and for the borrowers (the bond issuers), a higher rating means paying a lower interest rate on the debt. During a bull market, I recommend holding a portfolio of eighty percent stocks and twenty percent bonds and during a bear market I recommend holding a portfolio of eighty percent bonds and twenty percent stocks.

Although bonds are considered a safer investment, they do come with risks. When you purchase a bond, coupon rates are out of the investors control and may fluctuate. The coupon rates are controlled by the U.S. Treasury, The Federal Reserve, and the banking industry.

For Example:

The US Treasury issuing a bond will issue the bond with these variables; this will determine the investor rate of return on investment.

Coupon period - coupon rate (%) - maturity date - face value

The coupon period, coupon rate and maturity date are usually fixed, the face value may change but is usually fixed.

FOREX:

Foreign Exchange or Forex market is the world's largest financial market. Everyday trillions of dollars are exchanged from one currency to another, this type of currency exchange is needed for doing international business. Forex is an entity that I have questions about and is often challenged with some answers I have received.

Business use the Forex Market to do International Trade, when doing business with other people from across the world. When trading with Forex, you are trading two currencies against each other this is known as a "currency pair". For example, EUR-USD is the Euro trading against the US dollar. So, if the EUR-USD is trading at 1.15 this means that 1 Euro is equal to 1.15 US dollar.

Let's also take a look at another example USD-JPY; this is the United States dollar trading against the Japanese Yen. Therefore, if USD-JPY is trading at 110.20. This means that one United States dollar is equal to 110.20 Japanese Yen. Even though the pair is the EUR-USD, this act like a single entity, like a stock or futures. Investors profit from a stock when they buy a currency pair, when they buy and the price increase or when they short (sell), and the price decreases.

Currency pairs trade in specific quantities known as lots. They are standard lots, mini lots, and micro lots. Standard lots represent 100,000 units, mini lots represent 10,000 units and micro lots represent 1000 units. When trading on margin in Forex trading can only be covered from the funds already in the trader's account. Forex traders can't borrow money from the broker. Margin requirements can be as small as two percent of a trade or twenty percent of a trade. Most margin requirements for Forex Pairs are between three to five percent.

For example, an investor (trader) wants to buy the pair

USD-JPY and wanted to buy a standard lot of 1 unit. The total cost of the trade would be 110.20* 100,000 and the total cost of the trade would be 11,020,000 Japanese Yen or $100,000 United States dollars. This would mean that the investor needed one hundred thousand United States dollars in there brokers account to cover the trade. However, the investor does not have to pay that amount because of a margin. Let's say the margin requirement is five percent; five percent of one hundred thousand is five thousand. Therefore, the investor would only need five thousand in his/her Forex account to make this trade. Having leverage enables traders to control a large investment with a small amount of money in the example above the trader is able to control a $100,000 United States dollar investment with only $5000 in his/her account.

THE FIVE DOLLAR BILL

DERIVATIVES:

A derivative is the collective term used for several financial instruments whose value is based on something else and whose price is obtained from the performance of other underlying investments (these investments can be either shares or stocks, bonds, market indices, currencies, and commodities). Other security value is determined by, or derived from, the value of another asset.

Derivatives have two main uses. The first is to hedge risk to minimize the risk in the financial market. For example, if a corn producer (seller) thinks the price of corn will go up and the corn manufacturer (buyer) thinks the price will go down. They come to an agreement and say I will sell you 1 bushel of corn at the current market price of $10 in 8 months, regardless of the future market price. By locking in the price of corn, the buyer and seller are both protecting themselves. They both think the market price will be going a different way. If the price of corn falls in the next 8 months, the corn manufacturer (buyer) will wish they never had made that agreement.

They could have been buying corn cheaper and vice versa for the corn producer (seller), this is a zero-sum game where both the interest of the buyer and seller can be met. The second main uses for derivatives are for speculation, these derivatives are motivated by profit, rather than a desire to mitigate risk. Hedgers seek to limit risk by using derivatives as financial protection thus indirectly increasing profits while on the other hand, speculators are directly driven by the opportunity for profit.

There are four (4) main types of derivatives forwards, futures, swaps, and options. Forwards are customized contracts between two (2) parties to buy and sell an asset at a specified price at a specified future date. Forwards are not traded on a central exchange and as a result they're not standardized or regulated making them especially useful for hedging. Futures derivatives are similar to forwards but are standardized and regulated and are used to speculate on commodities. An Options derivative contract gives the right to an investor but not the obligation to buy(call) or sell (put) a security or other financial asset at a known price in a known pre-defined time frame. Options are an alternative way to speculate on the performance of a security, such as a stock or ETF.

Trading options is simple but there are a few terms you need to know when trading options. The expiration date on an options derivative is the date an option's final value is determined and can no longer be traded. Stocks usually have options with expiration dates ranging from a few days to a few years away. The strike price of an option derivative is the price at which shares will be bought or sold if an option derivative is exercised. The Option contract multiplier is the number of shares an option contract can be converted into.

A Swap derivative is the exchange of one security for another security, it allows you to change your exposure to something without having you getting your hands dirty, this could be a currency, interest rate or even an asset class based on several factors. There is another use of derivatives which is less popular but is used by mostly the wealthy and it is called arbitrage, which is the simultaneous buying and selling of securities, currency, or commodities in different markets. Most of these are in derivative forms in order to take advantage of differing prices for the same asset. This can be perceived as taking advantage of short-term price anomalies. For example, buying a product in one country for a cheaper price and importing it in another country and selling it for much more. Taking advantage of the price anomaly in one financial market of a product and selling it for a higher price in another market. Buying for low and selling high and this can be done on all financial markets with different products.

Derivatives trading has a lot of arguments for and against, in the financial market. The arguments for trading derivatives include Hedging Risk Exposure, Higher Returns and Underlying asset price determination, While the arguments against trading derivatives are speculative features and high volatility. Jobs do not have any future, but people do. I advise new traders to gain enough experience and knowledge on derivative trading instruments as these can bring nice colossal benefits

Entrepreneurs pop up in all types of industries and

can have widely different backgrounds. Some have built personal brands, while others work tirelessly on a physical product that they believe in. The one and five in multiples can become your best friends.

When starting your business, you must first begin with a clear goal and the steps you will take to achieve this goal. Never assume that your goals are too big. Think big and think positive and avoid limitations.

Any business you are starting, the first course you need to take is a course in sales, communication, and persuasion. These are skills that should be taught in a personalized manner. They cannot stress enough about teaching them in colleges and universities.

One of the most, if not" the most" important thing to do is to learn to influence and persuade a person you are selling your business products and services to. You will always need a strategy to develop your business. These strategies are vitally important and will come into play. You need a vision for your business that inspires you. Your standards should be congruent to your vision, and you should be able to communicate that vision with people to get them going and get them interested in your products or services from business.

My first business was a catering company and how I got sales was because of my ability to sell. I had contracts from several big-name companies in the industry even though I was a complete novice; my ability to sell put me over the top. Achievements of any kind is the crown of effort. No matter what you do you will have some people who love you and then on the other hand, the haters who will hate on whatever you do. Never mind them, focusing on your goals are your major concern. Who you surround yourself in your business will impact you? You need smart ethical business minded people like yourself to grow you as a person and grow your business.

Everyone should take risk and fail; you will learn more from failing than being successful in business. Consider your daily habits; would you use your own products and services. Your ideas must be usable to everyday people on a daily basis. There is no substitute for hard work and planning. People say luck, but the harder you work is the luckier you get. Think about your business how you want to take it to the next level and how you want to improve your products and services. Work very hard to classify what your purpose is, and make sure to clarify it in a straightforward sentence. The way you build great companies is with an infinite mindset by prioritizing people before profit and before resources. Of course, money does matter because it gives you options and provide resources, but people matter more.

Generating wealth is a lifelong game but your life is not a game it is real and should be enjoyed, all of it therefore you must begin right now, today with rewiring your mind and creating great wealth creating habits. Investing is not easy, but you need to master the rules first. Getting your mind right first, then profits later. Getting focused after you rewire your mind to generate real wealth will be a very important habit to have. Keeping focus is of utmost importance it aids you in achieving your goals.

All wealth generating skills are learnable. You can take a street cleaner, and that individual can learn skills to create wealth. Learning one skill at a time and putting focus on that important skill that will move there life forward.

I am here to teach you what the wealthy don't want you to know because nobody else is ever coming to save you. Get to work, you have far too many opportunities and potential in the richest country and economy in the world. It is by only patience and persistence that we as humans can get all the knowledge, we need to become wealthy. Creating wealth and living the life you deserve is waiting for you to continue procrastinating.

The greatest thing in the world is to be of service to others. There can be no progress without sacrifice. The world success will be how much one sacrifices. Our income is in the hands of others and is given to us through services we have rendered, with at least sixty percent of our time within a week of labor.

Human beings should stop falling in line and take a number; we are not animals we are different; We possess things that makes us different from all other creatures and this is priceless. We have the most valuable resource given to us at birth and that is your mind, yourself, you are your own individual self and your own person. God made you special and important and the act of withholding this truth or any truth is a lie.

A human being is literally what they think about. If you accept anything about life that is what you get. However, if you refuse to accept nothing but the best, that is exactly what you will get. You must always simply begin by setting your mind and heart upon it. I learned that if you truly want to achieve it you will. Circumstances does not make the man it reveals him. The body is the servant of the mind, and it obeys the orders of the mind, whether it be done consciously and intentionally or done spontaneously without conscious thought or intention.

Your mind and the thoughts that come from it are the fountains of your life that flows like a stream. Make the thoughts pure and good and the stream of life will flow with abundance and great purity. Clean thoughts create clean healthy body and bad thoughts do the opposite. Just as good thoughts bear good fruits thus bad thoughts bear bad fruits. As a physical weak out of shape individual can become strong through exercising, thus a weak-minded individual can train the mind and the thoughts and therefore become a strong minded individual by beginning to think with purpose and by making all conditions serve them. As the trees you are seeing growing outside sprung from a seed and could not have sprung without the seed, so everything thing you do whether good or bad springs from the hidden seeds of thought and could not have appeared without those thoughts.

There are remarkable elements in the life of everyone. You are today where yesterday thoughts and actions have brought you. You will be tomorrow where today thoughts and actions take you. Your thoughts are always trending in your journey! This shows you that you cannot escape the results of your thoughts and your actions that follow. I know you may ask why people become the way they are, but it is without a doubt, we live by faith, or we don't live at all.

We often ask, why is this lady a millionaire and this man is just a postal worker, it all is summed up into one statement. We become what we think about, we are today, the sum total of our thoughts. We are where we are because of what we think about, as we sow so shall we reap. It is very important to do the opposite of what the majority is doing. Most of us, if not all are followers and do not create our own path. Success is our journey not our destination. If you know what your goals are, you will know what you will become.

There is no freedom without discipline, by faith we can move mountains. Without faith we are nothing. Humans become great because they have the right mindset to do so. The human mind is extremely fertile and mysterious and does not care what we think about or what we plant. If we plant success we will reap success, the same way if we plant failure in our mind, we will reap failure. Plant your goal in your mind today! Know what is it that you want you want to be, a multi-millionaire, a world traveler, the best trader, or a top-notch salesman. All you have to do is plant that seed in your mind, water it and work on it and it will become yours. Take courage and believe in yourself to do it and know, there is no other way.

You can only earn money after you are successful, we have to be of service first before we have the money. Any person who contributes to prosperity must prosper in return. Act the part of the successful person you decide to be by becoming the person you want to become. A free human being is one that thinks for himself and not a crowd follower. The right time is now!

Today anything that can make life interesting, we should give more thought too. A good rule that always works for me is, whatever the majority is doing, I do the complete opposite and it has always worked for me. You should never follow the crowd or be a conformist to what the masses are doing. This is a sign they are controlled, and you have no full control of your own.

Ideas are the greatest things on earth; they are the things that change our minds. Your future represents great prospects for the individuals who have positive thoughts and ideas and who work towards their goals. Survival should never be the only course of action for human beings. It is in my opinion; it is of utmost importance that we enjoy our time on earth. God made us and this earth for us to enjoy, not to just be scraping and getting by. When someone succeeds everyone benefits; your family, friends, the community, and it goes on and on. Just remember in your everyday pursuit, a good idea attracts success and prosperity. The bigger, better and focus you are in your ideas, the more money it attracts. Success is not determined by the size of a person's brain, but only by the size of a person thoughts, each individual thinking. There is neither good nor bad, only thinking makes it either… I hope this book becomes your best friend and you will purchase more for your family and friends!!!

GLOSSARY

Arbitrage – This is the simultaneous buying and selling of securities, currency, or commodities in different markets mostly in derivative forms in order to take advantage of differing prices for the same asset this is really taking advantage of short-term price anomalies.

Chicago Mercantile Exchange (CME) – The Chicago Mercantile Exchange is a global derivatives marketplace based in Chicago. CME Group trades in agricultural products, currencies, energy, interest rates, metals, stock indexes, and weather. Individuals can register to trade through the CME group.

Commodity – This is a raw material or primary agricultural product that has full or substantial fungibility and can be traded, bought, or sold such as gold, platinum, silver, crude oil, soybean, corn, and livestock.

Consumer Price Index (CPI) – measures the average change in prices over time that consumers pay for a basket of goods and services.

Coupon – A coupon payment on a bond is the annual interest payment that the bondholder receives from the bond's issue date until it matures. A bond's coupon rate is expressed as a percentage of its par value.

Crypto currency – This is a digital or virtual currency that is secured by cryptography in which transactions are verified and records maintained by a decentralized system based on blockchain technology.

Gross Domestic Product (GDP) – the total value of goods produced, and services provided in a country for one year.

Derivative – A derivative is the collective term used for several financial instruments whose value is based on something else and whose price is obtained from or is dependent on the performance of other underlying investments (these investments can be either shares or stocks, bonds, market indices, currencies, and commodities) or any security whose value is determined by, or derived from, the value of another asset.

Dow Jones Industrial Average (Dow Jones or Dow) – This is a price-weighted measurement stock market index of 30 prominent companies listed on stock exchanges in the United States

Fiat money – Fiat money is a currency established as money, often by government regulation. Fiat money gives central banks greater control over the economy because they can control how much money is printed. Fiat money does not have intrinsic value and does not have use value and is not backed by a commodity such as gold.

Forex – The foreign exchange market is a global decentralized or over-the-counter market for the trading of currencies. Currencies are traded in pairs, so by exchanging one currency for another, a trader is speculating on whether one currency will rise or fall in value against the other.

Futures market/trading – This is an auction market in which participants buy and sell commodity and futures contracts for delivery on a specified future date at an agreed price between the buyer and the seller.

Nasdaq Composite – Nasdaq is a global electronic marketplace for buying and trading securities. It was the world's first electronic exchange and an index of more than 3,000 stocks listed on the Nasdaq exchange. Most of the world's technology giants, including Apple and Facebook, are listed on the Nasdaq.

Nonfarm Payrolls – This is the measure of the number of workers in the U.S. excluding farm workers and workers in a handful of other job classifications. This is measured by the Bureau of Labor Statistics (BLS), which surveys private and government entities throughout the U.S. about their payrolls.

OPEC – The Organization of the Petroleum Exporting Countries (OPEC) is a permanent, intergovernmental Organization, created at the Baghdad Conference on September 10–14, 1960, by Iran, Iraq, Kuwait, Saudi Arabia, and Venezuela.

Producer Price Index (PPI) – measures the average changes in prices received by domestic producers for their output.

Resistance – is a price level where an uptrend can be expected to pause due to a concentration of selling interest when prices have increased.

Securities and Exchange Commission (SEC) – The U.S. Securities and Exchange Commission is a large independent agency of the United States federal government, created in the aftermath of the Wall Street Crash of 1929, it was founded June 6, 1934. The purpose of the SEC is to enforce the law against market manipulation, protecting investors, maintaining fair and orderly functioning of the securities markets, and facilitating capital formation.

Standard and Poor's 500 (S&P 500) – This is a stock market index tracking the performance of 500 large companies listed on stock exchanges in the United States.

Support – This refers to prices on a chart that tend to act as a floor by preventing the price of an asset from being pushed downward.

ABOUT THE AUTHOR

Joshua Matthew Chronicles was born in Jamaica and migrated to the United States of America. Chronicles holds a bachelor's degree in international business and Finance and a master's degree in software development. Joshua Chronicles is also a Notary Public. The goal of this book is to be an all-time best seller in its field, and it foretells how Chronicles became more successful in his own right. Chronicles is popular among the retail trading community and has worked with companies, government entities and non-profit organizations in the areas of finance, training, logistics and management. His sole assignment now is to emancipate the millions if not billions who just live from paycheck to paycheck or hand to mouth kind of living, the desire to demonstrate to my readers by evidence of the success. Chronicles share factual arguments that are true and existing that you can achieve to live a prosperous, abundant filled and successful life. Chronicles has been featured in local and international magazines and plans to launch a non-profit organization to help impoverish kids in Africa.

Made in the USA
Monee, IL
04 November 2026

67381309R00059